DEDICATION

To my dear friend and colleague, Millie, who lived the spirit of Christmas in her heart every day. Your joy, kindness, and faith continue to inspire all who knew you. This book is dedicated to your memory, with love and gratitude for all the light you brought into the world.

Forward

Welcome to "Follow the Star: A Children's Nativity Story In 15 Stations" This devotional is designed to help children and families explore the beautiful story of Jesus' birth in a special way. Each station will guide you through moments leading up to and following that holy night in Bethlehem. Whether you're reading this together or reflecting on it individually, our hope is that these Stations bring you closer to the true meaning of Christmas.

Introduction

The story of Jesus' birth is a story of hope, love, and joy. In this devotional, we'll walk step by step through 15 Stations that tell this story. You'll discover how God prepared the world for Jesus and how people like Mary, Joseph, the Shepherds, and the Wisemen were part of His plan. Each station includes a short reading, a reflection, and a prayer. You'll also find artwork to help you imagine what it was like to be there that first Christmas.

Instructions on How to Use the Devotional

Choose A Time:
Find a quiet moment during the day or evening to go through one station. You can do one a day leading up to Christmas or at your own pace.

Begin With The Prayer:
Each station starts with the same opening prayer to help you focus and invite Jesus into your heart.

Look At The Artwork:
Spend a few moments looking at the picture. What do you notice? How does it make you feel? This will help you connect with the story.

Read and Reflect:
Read the short passage and reflection. Think about what it means and how it relates to your life.

Pray:
Use the prayer provided or say your own prayer. Ask God to help you understand and live the lessons of each station.

Dear Parents,

Thank you for choosing "Follow the Star: A Children's Nativity Story In 15 Stations" This devotional is designed to help your child grow in faith and understanding of the true meaning of Christmas. We encourage you to join your child in this journey by discussing the stories and reflections together. These moments can become a special part of your family's Christmas traditions, deepening your connection to the Nativity story and to each other.

May this book bless your family with peace, joy, and a renewed sense of wonder at the miracle of Christmas.

Dear Young People:
I'm so excited you're here! This book is all about the Christmas story, but in a way that's just for you. Together, we'll visit 15 special places called stations, where we'll learn more about Jesus' birth.
There will be pictures to look at, stories to read, and prayers to say.
I hope you'll have fun and discover how much God loves you.
Let's get started on our adventure to Bethlehem!

The First Station
Adam & Eve Disobey God

The First Station
Adam & Eve Disoebey God

"Opening Prayer: Jesus, Our Salvation, We Thank And Praise You."

Art From The Heart:

This picture shows Adam and Eve leaving the beautiful garden because they disobeyed God. Even though they made a mistake, God promised to send a Savior to make everything whole again. The picture helps us remember that God always has a plan, even when things go wrong.

God's Word: (Genesis 3:15)

"And I will put enmity between you and the woman and between your offspring and hers; he will crush your head, and you will strike his heel."

Think About It:

When Adam and Eve made a mistake, God didn't leave them alone. Instead, He promised to send Someone who would make things right again. This promise gives us hope that God never gives up on us, no matter what.

Just You And I Lord:

Dear God, thank You for loving us even when we make mistakes. Help us trust in Your promise and follow You every day. Guide us to make good choices and remember that You are always with us.

Echoes Of Grace:

"In our mistakes, God's love is true,
He promised a Savior for me and you."

Follow The Star:

How can you trust that God's love is always with you, even when you make mistakes?

The Second Station
Abraham's Promise

The Second Station
Abraham's Promise

"Opening Prayer: Jesus, Our Salvation, We Thank And Praise You."

Art From The Heart:

This picture shows Abraham trusting God, even when it was really hard.
God promised Abraham that through his family, the whole world would be blessed.
The picture reminds us that trusting God can lead to amazing things.

God's Word: (Genesis 22:18)

"And through your offspring, all nations on earth will be blessed,
because you have obeyed me."

Think About It:

God asked Abraham to trust Him, and because Abraham did, God blessed him
and his family. This teaches us that when we trust God,
He will guide us and bless us in ways we might not expect.

Just You And I Lord:

Dear God, thank You for Your promises and blessings. Help us to trust You
like Abraham did, even when it's difficult. Show us how to follow Your plan for our lives.

Echoes Of Grace:

"God promised Abraham blessings to see,
Through trust in Him, we are free."

Follow the Star:

How can you show trust in God, even when things are hard?

The Third Station
Jacob's Star

The Third Station
Jacob's Star

"Opening Prayer: Jesus, Our Salvation, We Thank And Praise You."

Art From The Heart:

This artwork shows Jacob dreaming of a ladder reaching
heaven, with angels going up and down.
God promised that a star would rise from Jacob's family, leading to the Savior.
The picture helps us think about how God's promises are like a light guiding us.

God's Word: (Numbers 24:17)

"I see him, but not now; I behold him, but not near.
A star will come out of Jacob; a scepter will rise out of Israel."

Think About It:

God showed Jacob that his family would be special, leading to the Savior.
Just like the star, God's promises shine bright and guide us.
We can trust that God's light will always show us the way.

Just You And I Lord:

Dear God, thank You for shining Your light on us through Your promises.
Help us follow the light of Jesus in our lives and trust in Your guidance every day.

Echoes Of Grace:

"A star will rise from Jacob's line,
Leading us to love divine."

Follow The Star:

How can you follow God's light in your life?

The Fourth Station
King David's Promise

The Fourth Station
King David's Promise

"Opening Prayer: Jesus, Our Salvation, We Thank And Praise You."

Art From The Heart:
This picture shows David, who was both a shepherd and a king. God promised David that one day, a King from his family would rule forever. The artwork reminds us that Jesus is the Good Shepherd and the King who loves and cares for us.

God's Word 2 (Samuel 7:12-13)
"When your days are over and you rest with your ancestors, I will raise up your offspring to succeed you, your own flesh and blood, and I will establish his kingdom."

Think About It:
David was chosen by God, and from his family came Jesus, our forever King. This teaches us that God's promises last forever and that Jesus is always with us, leading us and caring for us.

Just You And I Lord
Dear God, thank You for sending Jesus, the King who loves us forever. Help us to follow Him and trust in Your everlasting promises. Guide us to share Your love with others.

Echos Of Grace
"From David's line, a King did come, To lead us home, God's only Son."

Follow The Star:
How can you let Jesus, the Good Shepherd and King, lead you every day?

The Fifth Station
Prophecy of Emmanuel

The Fifth Station
Prophecy of Emmanuel

"Opening Prayer: Jesus, Our Salvation, We Thank And Praise You."

Art From The Heart

This picture shows the angel telling Mary that she would have a special baby named Jesus. The name "Emmanuel" means "God with us." The artwork reminds us that God loves us so much. He came to be with us in person through Jesus.

God's Word: Isaiah 7:14

"Therefore the Lord Himself will give you a sign:
The virgin will conceive and give birth to a Son and call him Emmanuel."

Think About It:

Long before Jesus was born, God promised through the prophet Isaiah that He would come to be with us. Jesus, called Emmanuel, shows us that God is always with us, loving and guiding us every day.

Just You And I Lord:

Dear God, thank You for being with us through Jesus, Emmanuel. Help us to feel Your presence in our lives and trust that You are always near. Show us how to share Your love with others.

Echoes Of Grace:

"Emmanuel, God's love so near,
In Jesus, we have nothing to fear."

Follow TheStar:

How can you remember that God is always with you, even in difficult times?

The Sixth Station
The Jesse Tree

The Sixth Station
The Jesse Tree

"Opening Prayer: Jesus, Our Salvation, We Thank And Praise You."

Art From The Heart:
This artwork shows the Jesse Tree, which tells the story of Jesus' family. From Jesse's family grew a small branch, and that branch was Jesus. The picture reminds us that God's love grows in our lives, even from small beginnings.

Scripture Passage: (Isaiah 11:1)
"A shoot will come up from the stump of Jesse; from his roots, a Branch will bear fruit."

Think About It:
God promised that a special branch would grow from Jesse's family, and that branch was Jesus. Just like a small plant grows into something big, God's love grows in us, too. We can trust that God is always working in our lives, even when we can't see it yet.

Just You and I Lord:
Dear God, thank You for growing Your love in our lives, just like You promised with the Branch of Jesse. Help us trust that even small things can grow into something great. Guide us in following You and watching Your plans grow in our lives.

Echoes Of Gace:
"A branch from Jesse, small and bright,
Grew into Jesus, our guiding light."

Follow The Star:
How can you trust that even small things in your life can grow into something amazing with God's help?

The Seventh Station
Humble Bethlehem

The Seventh Station
Humble Bethlehem

"Opening Prayer: Jesus, Our Salvation, We Thank And Praise You."

Art From The Heart:
This picture shows Bethlehem, a small town where Jesus was born. It wasn't a big or fancy place, but it became the most special place because Jesus was born there. The artwork reminds us that God can make even the smallest places and moments important.

Scripture Passage: Micah 5:2
"But you, Bethlehem Ephrathah, though you are small among the clans of Judah, out of you will come for Me, One who will be ruler over Israel, whose origins are from of old, from ancient times."

Think About It:
Bethlehem was a small and humble town, but it became famous because Jesus was born there. This shows us that God can make even small and humble things important. We can trust that God sees value in us, no matter where we are or what we do.

Just You And I Lord:
Dear Jesus, thank you for coming to a small town like Bethlehem. Help me remember that you can use even small things to do great work in the world. Amen."

Echoes Of Grace:
Bethlehem, so small and bright,
Gave the world its guiding light."

Follow The Star:
How can you remember that God sees value in you, no matter where you come from or how small you might feel?

The Eighth Station
Gabriel's Visit

The Eighth Station
Gabriel's Visit

"Opening Prayer: Jesus, Our Salvation, We Thank And Praise You."

Art From The Heart:

This picture shows the angel Gabriel visiting Mary to tell her that she will be the mother of Jesus. Mary is surprised, but she listens and says "Yes" to God. The artwork reminds us that God sometimes asks us to do surprising things, but He is always with us.

God's Word (Luke 1:26-28)

"In the sixth month of Elizabeth's pregnancy, God sent the angel Gabriel to Nazareth, a town in Galilee, to a virgin pledged to be married to a man named Joseph, a descendant of David. The virgin's name was Mary. The angel went to her and said, ' Greetings, you who are highly favored! The Lord is with you.'"

Think About It:

Mary was young and probably scared when the angel Gabriel visited her, but she trusted God and said "Yes." This teaches us that even when we feel unsure or scared, we can trust God's plan for us.

Just You And Me Lord:

Dear God, thank You for choosing Mary to be the mother of Jesus. Help us to trust in Your plan for our lives, even when we are unsure or scared. Give us the courage to say "yes" to You, just like Mary did.

Echoes Of Grace:

"Mary said yes, though she felt small, with God's help, she gave her all."

Follow The Star:

How can you say yes to God's plan, even when it feels surprising or scary?

The Nineth Station
A Baby's Joy

The Nineth Station
A Baby's Joy

"Opening Prayer: Jesus, Our Salvation, We Thank And Praise You."

Art From The Heart:

This picture shows Mary visiting her cousin Elizabeth, who is also expecting a special baby. When they meet, Elizabeth's baby leaps with joy. The artwork reminds us that when we share God's love with others, it brings joy to everyone.

God's Word: (Luke 1:39-41)

"At that time Mary got ready and hurried to a town in the hill country of Judea, where she entered Zechariah's home and greeted Elizabeth. When Elizabeth heard Mary's greeting, the baby leaped in her womb, and Elizabeth was filled with the Holy Spirit."

Think About It:

When Mary visited Elizabeth, they shared their joy and excitement about what God was doing in their lives. This reminds us that sharing God's love with others can bring happiness and encouragement. Just like Mary and Elizabeth, we can celebrate God's blessings together.

Just You And I Lord:

Dear God, thank You for the friendship between Mary and Elizabeth. Help us to share Your love and joy with others, just like they did. Teach us to celebrate Your blessings in our lives and in the lives of others.

Echoes Of Grace:

"Mary and Elizabeth, the joy they share,
God's love is shown, everywhere."

Follow The Star:

How can you share God's love and joy with others, like Mary and Elizabeth did?

The Tenth Station
Jesus' Birth

The Tenth Station
Jesus' Birth

"Opening Prayer: Jesus, Our Salvation, We Thank And Praise You."

Art From The Heart:
This picture shows the special night when Jesus was born in a stable in Bethlehem. There were no fancy places for Him, just a humble manger. The artwork reminds us that Jesus came to us in a simple way, showing that God's love is for everyone.

Scripture Passage: Luke 2:6-7
"While they were there, the time came for the Baby to be born, and she gave birth to her firstborn, a Son. She wrapped Him in cloths and placed Him in a manger because there was no guest room available for them."

Think About It:
Jesus was born in a simple, humble place, but He brought the greatest gift of all—God's love for us. This teaches us that God's love doesn't need to be fancy or big. It can come in small, quiet moments, and it is for everyone, no matter where they are.

Just You And I Lord:
Dear God, thank You for sending Jesus to be born in a humble place. Help us to see Your love in the simple and quiet moments of our lives. Remind us that Your love is for everyone, no matter where we are or who we are.

Echoes Of Grace:
"In a stable, Love was born,
A humble King, no crown worn."

Follow The Star:
How can you find God's love in the simple, quiet moments of your life?

The Eleventh Station
Angel's Good News

The Eleventh Station
Angel's Good News

"Opening Prayer: Jesus, Our Salvation, We Thank And Praise You."

Art From The Heart

This picture shows angels announcing Jesus' birth to shepherds in the fields. The shepherds were just ordinary people, but God chose them to hear the good news first.
The artwork reminds us that God's message is for everyone, no matter who they are.

God's Word: Luke 2:8-9

"And there were shepherds living out in the fields nearby, keeping watch over their flocks at night. An angel of the Lord appeared to them, and the glory of the Lord shone around them, and they were terrified."

Think About It:

The angels announced Jesus' birth to shepherds, who were not important or famous.
This shows us that God's love is for everyone, no matter who they are.
We can share God's message with others, just like the angels did.

Just You And I Lord:

Dear God, thank You for sharing the good news with everyone, no matter who they are.
Help us to be like the angels and share Your love with others.
Teach us to see that everyone is important to You.

Echoes Of Grace:

"Angels sang to shepherds low,
God's great love for all to know."

Follow The Star:

How can you share God's message of love with others, like the angels did?

The Twelveth Station
Follow That Star

The Twelveth Station
Follow That Star

"Opening Prayer: Jesus, Our Salvation, We Thank And Praise You."

Art From The Heart:

This picture shows the Wisemen visiting Jesus with gifts. They traveled a long way, following a star, to find the newborn King. The artwork reminds us that when we seek God, He will guide us, just like He guided the Wisemen.

God's Word: (Matthew 2:9-11)

"After they had heard the king, they went on their way, and the star they had seen when it rose went ahead of them until it stopped over the place where the child was. When they saw the star, they were overjoyed. On coming to the house, they saw the child with his mother Mary, and they bowed down and worshiped him. Then they opened their treasures and presented him with gifts of gold, frankincense, and myrrh."

Think About It:

The Wisemen traveled far to find Jesus and bring Him gifts. This teaches us that when we look for God, He will show us the way. We can also bring our own gifts to Jesus—our love, our kindness, and our hearts.

Just You And I Lord:

Dear God, thank You for guiding the Wisemen to Jesus. Help us to seek You are in our lives and we offer You the best gift we have - our love for You.

Echoes Of Grace

"Wise Men followed the star so bright,
Bringing gifts to the Savior's light."

Follow The Star:

What gifts can you bring to Jesus, just like the Wise Men did?

The Thirteenth Station
Temple Blessing

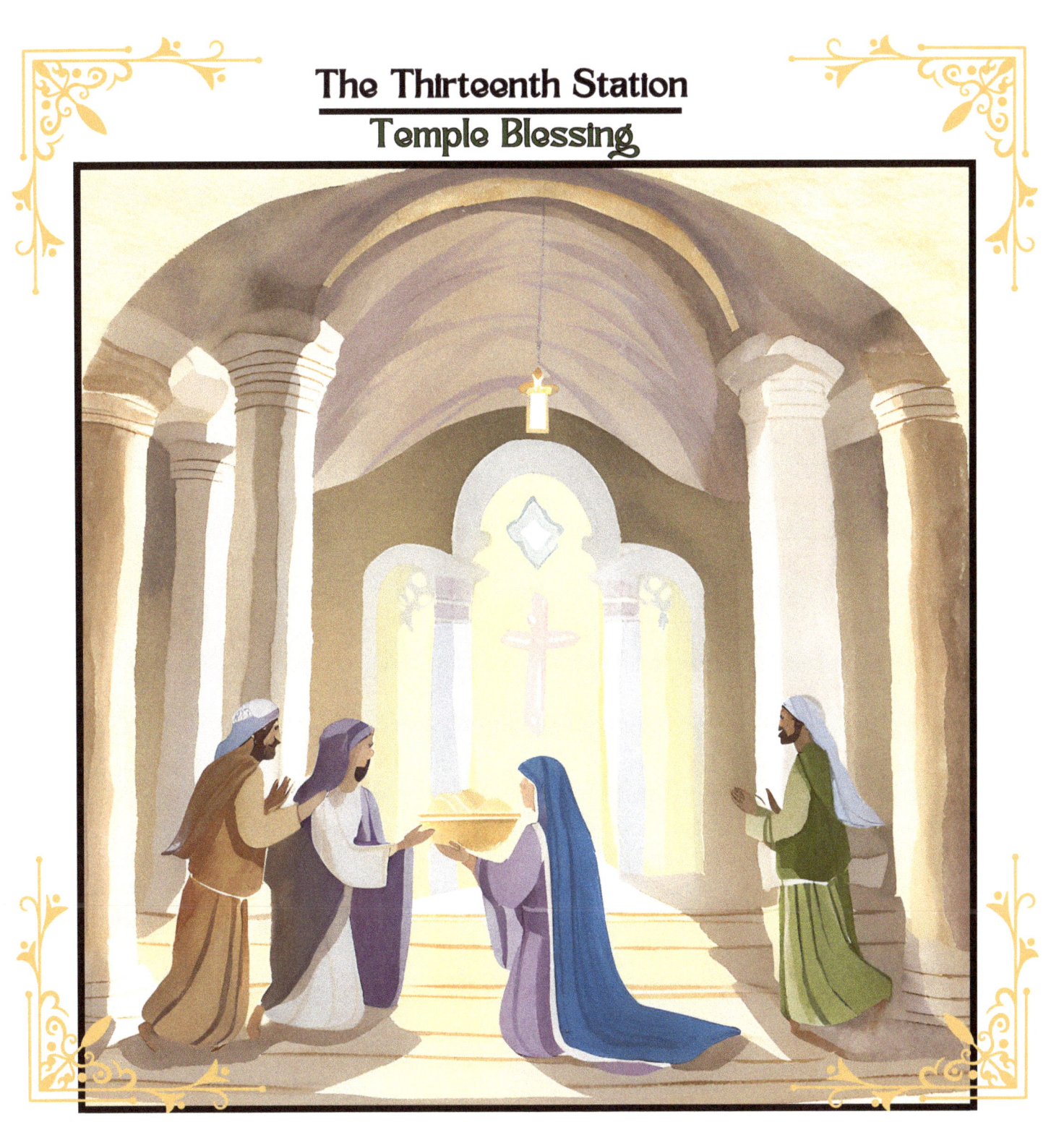

The Thirteenth Station
Temple Blessing

"Opening Prayer: Jesus, Our Salvation, We Thank And Praise You."

Art From The Heart:
This picture shows Mary and Joseph bringing baby Jesus to the temple, where Simeon and Anna recognize Him as the Savior. The artwork reminds us that Jesus was dedicated to God, and we can dedicate our lives to Him too.

Scripture Passage: (Luke 2:22-24)
"When the time came for the purification rites required by the Law of Moses, Joseph and Mary took him to Jerusalem to present him to the Lord (as it is written in the Law of the Lord, 'Every firstborn male is to be consecrated to the Lord'), and to offer a sacrifice in keeping with what is said in the Law of the Lord: 'a pair of doves or two young pigeons.'"

Think About It:
When Mary and Joseph brought Jesus to the temple, they dedicated Him to God. This shows us that Jesus belongs to God, and we do too. We can dedicate our lives to God.

Just You And I Lord:
Dear God, thank You for the example of Mary and Joseph, who dedicated Jesus to You. Help us to dedicate our lives to You, trusting in Your plan for us. Guide us as we live our lives for You, knowing that we belong to You.

Echoes Of Grace:
"In the temple, Jesus was blessed,
Dedicated to God's great quest."

Follow The Star:
How can you dedicate your life to God, trusting in His special plan for you?

The Fourteenth Station
Teaching In Temple

The Fourteenth Station
Teaching In Temple

Opening Prayer: Jesus, Our Salvation, We Thank And Praise You."

Art From The Heart:
This picture shows the young Jesus in the temple, sitting with the teachers and asking questions. Everyone was amazed at His wisdom, even though He was only twelve years old. The artwork reminds us that we can learn from Jesus, no matter how young we are. He teaches us about God and what it means to love others.

God's Word: (Luke 2:46-47)
"After three days they found him in the temple courts, sitting among the teachers, listening to them and asking them questions. Everyone who heard him was amazed at his understanding and his answers."

Think About It:
Even as a child, Jesus was wise and eager to learn about God. This teaches us that we can start learning about God at any age. Jesus wants us to grow in wisdom and love, just like He did. We can ask questions, learn, and share what we know with others.

Just You And Me Lord:
Dear God, thank You for Jesus, who showed us that we can always learn more about You. Help us to grow in wisdom and understanding, just like Jesus did.

Echoes Of Grace:
"Young Jesus, wise beyond His years,
Teaches love, without any fears."

Follow The Star:
How can you grow in wisdom and learn more about God, like Jesus did when He was a child?

The Fifteenth Station
Our Christmas Story

The Fifteenth Station
Our Christmas Story

"Opening Prayer: Jesus, Our Salvation, We Thank And Praise You."

Artwork From The Heart:
This artwork reminds us that the Nativity story is not just a historical event but a living reality that touches each of our lives. It encourages us to see ourselves as part of this sacred story, sharing in the joy and grace of Christ's birth.

Scripture Passage: John 1:14
"And the Word became flesh and lived among us, and we have seen His glory, the glory as of a Father's only Son, full of grace and truth."

Think About It:
John's words about the Word becoming flesh remind us that Jesus, who is God, came to live with us as a baby. The Nativity isn't just something that happened long ago—it's a reminder that Jesus is still with us everyday. Let us share His love and kindness We are all called to be part of His story, bringing His light to the world.

Just You And I Lord:
Lord, we are grateful that Jesus' birth invites us into the Nativity story. Help us to see ourselves as part of this sacred event, cherishing the grace and truth You offer.

Echoes Of Grace:
"In Christmas' light, we find our place,
Embraced by love, we share Your grace."

Follow The Star:
How can you actively embrace and share the grace and joy of the Nativity story in your own life and relationships?

Prayer Service, Pageant, And Presentation Suggestions

Turning the Stations of the Nativity into a Christmas pageant, musical, or prayer service can be an ongoing and meaningful way to teach and celebrate the Nativity Story.
Here are some suggestions for educators:

1. Christmas Pageant

Roles & Characters: Assign each of the 15 stations to a different group of students or individuals, representing characters like Adam and Eve, Abraham, Isaiah, the Holy Family, shepherds, etc. Costumes and simple props can enhance the storytelling.

Narration: Use reflective meditations, scripture readings, and personal prayers as the script for narrators to guide the audience through the Nativity journey.

Tableaux or Short Performances: For each station, consider a tableau or a brief acted-out scene that visually represents the story while a narrator reads the corresponding reflections and scripture.

Incorporating Music: Integrate traditional Christmas carols and hymns between stations, allowing the choir or audience to sing while transitioning between scenes.

2. Christmas Musical with a Choir

Choir Involvement: The choir can perform songs that align with the themes of each station. Songs like "O Come, O Come, Emmanuel" or "Silent Night" could be paired with specific reflections. Choir pieces can also be interwoven with the scripture readings.

Children's Participation: If working with younger students, one could have children sing or recite simplified prayers and reflections, with the choir providing more complex arrangements.

Creative Staging: Include a mix of live singing and narration, allowing each station's message to unfold through a blend of drama and music. For example, as the story of the shepherds is told, the choir could sing "The First Noel," by students or volunteers, connecting the Old Testament prophecies with the New Testament fulfillment.

Audience Participation: Have the audience join in for a repetitive refrain, like "Jesus, our salvation, we thank and praise you," after each station to foster engagement.

Art Display: If possible, display relevant artwork from the Stations of the Nativity in the background or on screens to reinforce the visual aspect of each station's meditation

Prayer Service, Pagent, And Presentation Suggestions

3. Prayer Service
Reverence and Reflection: For a more solemn approach, the Stations of the Nativity can be used as part of a prayer service where scripture is read aloud, followed by periods of reflection, meditative music, and group prayer. Prayer service suggestions:

Candle Lighting: Have a candle or small lantern available for each station. The last station should have all bearer(s) raise their lighting. A candle bearer can walk from station to station if a tableau setting is used. A candlelight ceremony can be part of the service environment.

Interactive Elements: Encourage participants to write down or share their personal prayers after each station, offering their reflections on how the Nativity story connects to their lives today.

Music for Contemplation: Include quiet, instrumental music during reflection periods to give participants a chance to pray silently or reflect on the station's message.

Additional Suggestions:
Integration with Scripture: Each station's scripture can be performed or read aloud by students or volunteers, connecting the Old Testament prophecies with the New Testament fulfillment.

Audience Participation: Have the audience join in for a repetitive refrain, like "Jesus, our salvation, we thank and praise you," after each station to foster engagement.

Art Display: If possible, display relevant artwork from the Stations of the Nativity in the background or on screens to reinforce the visual aspect of each station's meditation

The Hymn & Song Suggestions

Station One:..I Come To The Garden Alone
Station Two:...Come Thou Long Expected Jesus
Stations Three:...The First Noel
Station Four:..Hark The Herald Angels Sing
Station Five:...O Come O Come Emmanuel
Station Six:..Lo, How A Rose Er Blooming
Station Seven:...O Little Town Of Bethlehem
Station Eight:...Hail Mary, Gentle Woman
Station Nine:..On Jordan's Banks The Baptist Cry
Station Ten:...Silent Night
Station Eleven:...We Have Heard On High Angels
Station Twelve:..We Three Kings
Station Thirteen:...What Child Is This?
Station Fourteen:..Mary, Did You Know
Station Fifteen:...I Want To Walk As A Child Of The Light

More Tales From The StoryTeller Shop

© 2024 The Storyteller Shop

All rights reserved. No part of this publication may be reproduced, distributed, or transmitted in any form or by any means, including photocopying, recording, or other electronic or mechanical methods, without the prior written permission of the publisher, except in the case of brief quotations embodied in critical reviews and certain other noncommercial uses permitted by copyright law.

For permission requests, write to the publisher, addressed "Attention: Permissions Coordinator," at the address below:

The Storyteller Shop
www.thestoryellershop.com